Raspberry Pi 3

Setup, Programming and Developing Amazing Projects with Raspberry Pi for Beginners - With Source Code and Sep by Step Guides

This book is part of the series:

The Wonderful World of Engineering

1

Part I: Getting Started with the Raspberry Pi

The Raspberry Pi is a very common device all over the world. A lot of people young and old are using it to learn to program using of the common programming languages. The device is also widely used for playing computer games. Most Raspberry Pi users don't know that it can be used in multiple ways, including home automation. It will be good to enjoy maximum usage. This book is a guide for you on how to use the Raspberry Pi 3. You are guided from the basic steps of setting up the device to be ready for usage to utilizing to accomplish complex tasks.

If you have just acquired your Raspberry Pi and don't how to use it, this is the best guide. If you have been using a Raspberry Pi for basic tasks and you need to know how to maximize usage, this book will also be good for you. Have you ever wished to know how to program your Raspberry Pi with Python programming language? This book will guide you step by step. The examples given in this book are for Raspberry Pi 3, so ensure that you are using this version of the Pi device. Enjoy reading and enjoy developing!

Chapter 1 - What can I do with the Pi?

The Raspberry Pi is a single-board computer developed to help in teaching the basics of computer science in schools. Several models have been released, with the latest being the Raspberry Pi 3. The device can be applied in a lot of areas and it is commonly used by hackers, artists and students.

The following are a few of the uses of the Raspberry Pi:

1. **Retro gaming**
   The Raspberry Pi can be transformed into a retro game console to play games such as Sega, Nintendo, Arcade and GameBoy. Doing this will not take you more than 30 minutes.

2. **Raspberry Pi tablet**
   The Raspberry device can be transformed into a tablet using the RPi TouchScreen. This can also be done easily and you will get a good result.

3. **Desktop PC**
   You can setup your Raspberry Pi as a useful (although rather slow) desktop computer. However, you will be needed to have other items such as a mouse, screen, keyboard, and if possible, an extra storage device.

4. **Browsing the Web**
   You should also install an operating system available for the RPI such as Raspbian. You will get apps like email for web browsing.

5. **Cloud Server**

   You can transform your Rapberry Pi into a cloud server. You should install a software such as the ownCloud to be able to use the device for storing and accessing files. After setting up your cloud server, you will be able to store your files in your own private cloud storage.

6. **Raspberry Pi Cluster**

   You can build a "supercomputer" from the RPi boards. This is a cool and easy way to learn how to build clusters.

7. **Media Center**

   It is possible to run the media center application for the TV on your Raspberry Pi. This will allow you to organize and play media such as pictures, music, and videos.

8. **Web server**

   You can use your Raspberry pi device as a web server, although a lightweight one. It is capable of handling a small to medium amount of traffic; and you can use it to learn programming languages for the web such as PHP, CSS, HTML and MySQL. You can also use it to launch your own WordPress blog or website.

9. **VPN**

   A VPN (Virtual Private Network) helps you when you need to extend your private network into public places. It is good for a secure and encrypted Internet connection.

10. **PiPhone**

    you can use your Raspberry Pi to build a working phone.

11. **Home Automation System**

You can create a powerful home automation application from your Raspberry Pi. This can be done by attaching cameras, sensors, relays, and other devices to it. As a result, it will be possible for you to control your home from a remote location. You can add Arduinos to have extra functionalities.

Chapter 2 - How to Setup the Pi

In this chapter, we will be showing you how to setup the Raspberry Pi 3 device. To do the setup, you should have the following:

1. **Raspberry Pi**- make sure you have the Raspberry Pi 3 device.

2. An **HDMI monitor or television**- you will be expected to connect your Pi to a monitor, meaning that an HDMI-enabled screen will be needed.

3. A **USB mouse and keyboard**- these are paramount as they will help you control your Pi. Choose any USB mouse and keyboard.

4. A **card reader and 8GB MicroSD card**- rather than a hard drive, the operating system for the Pi should be installed on a MicroSD card. A card of a minimum of 8GB will be needed.

5. Power supply- a micro USB is usually used to power the Raspberry Pi. There are four ports on the Pi 3, so choose a power supply that can supply at least 2.5A.

Once you have all the above accessories, it will be time for you to get started setting up your Pi 3 device.

Using NOOBS to Install Raspbian OS onto SD Card

You should first install the Raspbian OS on the SD card. This is an indication that you should begin by downloading the operating system onto your computer and using a card reader to transfer it to an SD card.

There are two ways to achieve this. You can choose to do the installation of the Raspbian manually: you will use an external software or the command line tool. You may also choose to download then install NOOBS (New Out of Box Software). The latter is the simplest way to do it, so it's the one we will be using. Follow the steps given below:

1. Place the SD card in the computer or a SD card reader.

2. Download NOOBS. Choose the option for "offline and network install." The version will have Raspbian in the download.

3. The SD card may have to be formatted to support the FAT file format. Find a tutorial that guides you as it is beyond the scope of this book.

4. Extract the contents you have downloaded in a zipped format, then move them to a SD card. Once done, eject the SD card and plug it into your Raspberry Pi 3 device.

You will now be ready, and the rest of the work can be done on the Pi device. It is time for you to connect the monitor.

Connecting the Devices

It is easy to connect your devices to Raspberry Pi 3. However, this process should be done in an orderly manner so that the Pi 3 can recognize all the devices you attach.

You should begin by connecting the HDMI cable to the Raspberry Pi 3 and the monitor, and finally adding the USB devices. For those using an Ethernet cable to establish a connection to a router, just do it.

After you have connected everything, connect the power adapter. Raspberry Pi has no power switch, and it turns on automatically after you have connected it to the power supply.

Setting up the Raspbian

Once you boot up the NOOBS for the first time, it will take a few minutes to format the SD card then setup other things, so you have to give it time. A screen will be displayed asking you to install the operating system, which can be done as follows:

1. Move to the bottom of the screen, then choose the language you want to use as well as the keyboard layout you need based on your location.

2. Click on button next to the Raspbian, then on Install.

You should give the NOOBS time to install the Raspbian OS; it will take about 10 to 20 minutes. Once the process is complete, the system will restart and you will be taken to the desktop, and it is from here that you will be able to perform any necessary configuration. Congratulations, now you have "upgraded" your Raspberry Pi to a Raspbian Pi :-)

Configuring the Raspbian Pi

The Raspbian OS comes with a Start menu from which you can launch the file browser, open applications and everything you may need from your operating system. Begin by setting up a connection to the Wi-Fi network and any Bluetooth devices you may need.

Connecting to the Wi-Fi Network

The process of connecting a Raspbian OS is done in a similar manner as with the other modern operating systems. To connect to a Wi-Fi network, follow the steps below:

1. Move to top right corner of the screen, then click on network icon--the one with two computers.

2. Choose the name of the Wi-Fi to which you need to connect, then type in your password.

If you type the correct password, you will be connected to the Wi-Fi network directly. After setting up the Wi-Fi network, you will be able to use it from both the graphical user interface and the command line.

Connecting Bluetooth Devices

You may have Bluetooth devices such as the mouse and keyboard which you will need to connect to your Pi 3 device. In such a case, you have to pair this device with the Pi. The process is determined by the device you need to connect to your Pi, but the steps are straightforward:

1. Click on Bluetooth icon located on upper right corner of the screen.

2. Click on "Add Device."

3. Identify the device to which you need to connect, then click on it and follow the onscreen instructions to accomplish the pairing.

You must now connect your Raspberry Pi 3 to your Bluetooth device. You can play around with it and start to do what you want.

Chapter 3 - Establishing a Remote Connection

Connect to your Raspberry Pi 3

You can establish a connection to your Pi from a remote location. This becomes useful when you don't have a monitor or there is only a laptop in the house. The following are some of the ways you can establish a remote connection to your Pi:

Using SSH on the Command Line

It is possible for you to establish a connection to the command line of your Pi from your computer by using the SSH (Secure Shell). You will then be able to run any commands from your computer and they will be executed on your Pi. However, you will not be provided with the graphical user interface for the Raspberry Pi.

For those working on a project that doesn't expect you have access to the screen, this is the best approach to establish a connection to your Pi.

Let us discuss how you can connect to your Pi from a Mac OS or Linux computer, or just from another Raspberry Pi; you will not be required to install any additional software.

You should be aware of the IP address of your Raspberry Pi. To know this, open the terminal of the Pi and then run the following command:

```
hostname -I
```

If you are using the device without a screen, you can look for the device list on your router or use the nmap tool.

Now that you know the IP address of your Pi, you can run the following commands from your computer terminal:

```
ssh pi@<IP>
```

Note that in this case, the <IP> should be replaced with the IP address of your Pi. For those who get the "connection timed out" error, you have used the wrong IP address to connect.

If the connection runs successfully, you will see an authenticity/security warning. Type "yes" to continue. The warning should only be seen the first time for you to connect to your Pi via SSH.

In case your Pi has taken an IP address for a device that had been connected to your computer before, you will get a warning and prompted to clear the list of the known devices in your computer. Just follow the instructions and run the ssh command for the second time, which should now run successfully.

You will be prompted to enter the password for your Pi. The default password for the Raspbian is "raspberry." Afterward, the Raspberry Pi prompt will be presented to you, and you will notice that it is the same as the one you see on the Pi.

In case you have setup some other user on your Raspberry Pi, the connection should be done by following similar steps. If the connection runs successfully, you will see the following prompt:

```
pi@raspberrypi ~ $
```

You will then be connected to your Pi and are able to run the commands you need.

X-forwarding

You can choose to forward the X session via SSH, and this will enable you to make use of the graphical user applications by use of the –Y flag. The following demonstrates how this can be done:

```
ssh -Y pi@192.168.160.2
```

For Macs using OS X, the X11 is not provided, so be sure you download and install it.

At this point, you are using the command line tool, but it is possible for you to open the graphical user interface. To demonstrate this, run the following command:

```
idle3 &
```

The command will open editor IDLE for Python in a graphical window. If you type the command

```
scratch &
```

the Scratch will open up for you.

If you need to get more information regarding the ssh command, just type "man ssh" on the terminal.

Allowing SSH Access without a Password

It is possible for you to configure your Pi so that it will allow your computer to connect to it via SSH without the need to provide the password. To achieve this, you will have to generate a SSH key.

First check whether there are keys on your computer that you can use to establish a connection to your Raspberry Pi. You can see such keys by running the following command:

```
ls ~/.ssh
```

If you see files with the name "id_rsa.pub" or "id_dsa.pub," you will be have some keys already setup, so it is possible for you to skip the step for generating the SSH keys. If you want to generate other SSH keys, first delete these keys.

Below is the command you can run to generate the SSH keys.

Make sure that you use a hostname which makes sense like "<YOURNANME>@<YOURDEVICE>". Here is the command:

```
ssh-keygen -t rsa -C nicohsam@pi
```

Comments can be added and enclosed within quotes if there are spaces as shown below:

```
ssh-keygen -t rsa -C "Raspberry Pi #235"
```

Once you type the above command, you will asked to choose the location in which you need to save the key. It is good for you to save the key in the default location, which is /home/pi/.ssh/id_rsa, simply by pressing the Enter key.

You will also be prompted to type a passphrase. This is for security purposes as your key will be useless without this passphrase. This means in case someone else copies your key, it will be impossible for them to impersonate you and gain access to the Pi. If you are prompted, just type the passphrase, then retype it again if prompted, and hit the Enter key.

At this point you should be able to see "id_rsa" and "id_rsa.pub" files in the .ssh directory of the home folder. You must run the following command:

```
ls ~/.ssh
```

In my case, I get the following result:

```
authorized_keys  id_rsa  id_rsa.pub  known_hosts
```

The file "id_rsa" forms the private key. You should keep it in your computer.

The file named "id_rsa.pub" represents your public key. This is the key you should put on to machines to which you are in need of connecting. In case the public and the private keys are matched, the connection will run successfully. You can use the cat command to see the public key on your terminal as shown below:

```
cat ~/.ssh/id_rsa.pub
```

This key should be in the following form:

```
ssh-rsa <LONG STRING OF RANDOM CHARACTERS> nicohsam@pi
```

It is now time for you to copy the key from the computer to the Raspberry Pi. If there is no .ssh directory in your Pi, then you must create one as it will help you do the copying. This can be achieved by running the following command:

```
cd ~
install -d -m 700 ~/.ssh
```

For you to copy the public key to the Raspberry Pi, you must use the command given below to append your public key to the "authorized_keys" file on your Pi. Then send it over the SSH with this command:

```
cat ~/.ssh/id_rsa.pub | ssh <USERNAME>@<IP-ADDRESS> 'cat >>
.ssh/authorized_keys'
```

Note that in this case, you will have to perform authentication using your password. You can then run the "ssh <USER>@<IP-ADDRESS>" command and you will be allowed to establish a connection without being prompted to use a password.

However, you may get the "agent admitted failure to sign using the key" message. In this case, you will have to add DSA and RSA identities to your authentication agent and ssh-agent and execute the command given below:

```
ssh-add
```

If this fails to work, you will have to run the "rm ~/.ssh/id*" command to delete the keys, then follow the same steps. You can also use the secure copy (scp) command to send the files over SSH.

Virtual Network Computing (VNC)

Sometimes, working directly with the Pi becomes inconvenient. You may need to work on it from some other device by use of a remote control.

The VNC refers to a graphical desktop system for sharing and it can allow you to exercise control over a computer desktop (running a VNC server) from some other mobile device or computer (running VNC viewer).

The VNC Viewer will be responsible for transmitting keyboard and mouse touch events to the VNC Server, and the return will be getting updates on your screen.

With this, you will be able to see your Raspberry Pi's desktop inside the window of your mobile device or computer. You will be able to exercise control as if you were working on the Pi itself.

VNC Connect from the RealVNC comes included with the Raspbian. It provides you with both the VNC Server and the VNC Viewer. The VNC Server will allow you to control the Raspberry Pi remotely, while the VNC Viewer will allow you to control the desktop computers remotely from your Raspberry Pi if this is what you need.

The VNC Server should be enabled before it can be used. By default, it will give you remote access to your graphical desktop, which is running on the Raspberry Pi, and you will use it as if you are seated adjacent.

It is also possible for you to gain some graphical access to your Raspberry Pi in case it is not running some graphical desktop or it is headless.

Enabling the VNC Server

First ensure that you are using the latest version of the VNC Connect. Run the commands below:

```
sudo apt-get update
sudo apt-get install realvnc-vnc-server realvnc-vnc-viewer
```

These commands will help you update the system. You can then go ahead and enable the server, which can be done from the command line or through the graphical user interface.

To do this via the graphical user interface, first boot your Raspberry Pi 3 to its desktop. Next, navigate through "Menu > Preferences > Raspberry Pi Configuration > Interfaces". Make sure that the VNC has been enabled.

The "raspi-config" will allow you to enable your VNC server via the command line. Fun the following command:

```
sudo raspi-config
```

To enable the VNC server, do the following:

Navigate to the Interfacing Options.

Scroll down then choose "VNC > Yes".

Using the VNC Viewer to Connect to the Raspberry Pi

There are two ways you can connect to your Raspberry Pi. You can use one of them or both, and this will be determined by what is best for you.

Direct Connection

It is always easy to establish a direct connection to your Pi as long you are on the private local network. The connection can be done by use of a wired or wireless network either at home, school, or even an office.

You should begin by discovering the IP address by running the "ifconfig" command. Use the device you will need to use to take control over the Raspberry Pi and download the VNC Viewer.

Open the VNC Viewer, then type in the IP address of your Raspberry Pi.

Cloud Connection

You can use the cloud service of RealVNC for free, provided the remote access is done either for non-commercial or education purposes. Connections to the cloud are usually done in a convenient and encrypted manner from end-to-end. They are highly recommended for those who need to establish a connection to a Raspberry Pi over the Internet. You are not expected to configure either a router or a firewall, and it is not a must to be aware of the IP address of the Raspberry Pi, or give some static one.

Begin by creating your account with RealVNC, which is free. Use the credentials for this account to sign onto the VNC Server of your Raspberry Pi.

Download the VNC Viewer on the device from which you need to take control. You can then use the same credentials to sign in to your VNC Viewer, then click to establish a connection to the Raspberry Pi.

Authentication in VNC Server

To complete the cloud, or even a direct connection, you must perform the authentication in the VNC Server. If you are establishing the connection from a compatible VNC Viewer app and from the RealVNC, provide the username and the password which you normally use to log onto the user account on your Raspberry Pi. These credentials take a default of "pi" and "raspberry."

If you are establishing the connection from the non-RealVNC Viewer app, first you will have to downgrade the authentication scheme of your

VNC Server, give a password unique to the VNC Server, and enter it instead. On your Raspberry Pi, launch the dialog for the VNC Server by navigating through "Menu > Options > Security," then click on Authentication dropdown to choose "VNC Password."

Create a Virtual Desktop

For those using a headless Raspberry Pi, or one not connected to a monitor, it is less likely for it to be running a desktop.

With a VNC Server, you can create a desktop, which will give you some graphical remote access when you need it. The virtual desktop can be found in the memory of your Raspberry Pi. For you to create and establish a connection to the virtual desktop, perform the following:

Open the terminal of your Pi or establish a remote connection with SSH, then run the following command:

```
vncserver
```

An IP address will be printed on the terminal, so take note of this value.

Type the information into the VNC Viewer of the device you need to take control of. If you are in need of destroying your virtual desktop, execute the command below:

```
vncserver -kill :<display-number>
```

Any available connections to your desktop will also be stopped.

Chapter 4 - Turning Raspberry Pi 3 into a Media Center

You can transform your Raspberry Pi3 into a XBMC media center in a few minutes. Begin by assembling all the necessary materials. We will be guiding you how to do this. You should have the following materials:

4. A **Raspberry Pi 3**

    we will be using Model 3 of the Raspberry Pi for setup.

5. A **composite or HDMI video cable**

    this cable will facilitate the connection of your Raspberry Pi to a monitor or television.

6. **8GB Class 10 SD Card and a card reader**.

    If you have a better version of the SD card, you can use it as well. We are using the 8GB size for better performance.

7. **A USB mouse and keyboard**

    Choose any standard USB mouse and keyboard as they will work. Also, feel free to use a wireless keyboard and mouse, but note that you will reconnect them whenever your Raspberry Pi reboots.

8. **An Ethernet cable**

    feel free to use any standard one as it will work correctly.

9. **A micro USB power supply**

    It will be good for you to get one made specifically to be used with the Raspberry Pi. This will ensure that you don't get into problems. Some chargers for smartphones will work.

10. **A remote control**

You may not need to use a keyboard or a mouse for controlling the media center once it has been setup. In such a case, you should have a remote.

11. **USB hard drive**

This is optional and will help to store your videos if you are not in need of streaming the videos from other computers.

12. **A stereo audio cable, 3.5mm**

This is optional for those using an analog video and there is a need to connect the Raspberry Pi to a set of external speakers and internal ones on the monitor or television. For those using HDMI, feel free to skip this step.

13. **Raspbmc Installer**

This will help you put Raspbmc onto the SD card. Go to the official website for Raspbmc and get it for free.

Let's go

After you are done with what has been discussed in this chapter, you will get an XBMC box capable of playing a 720p video. Follow the steps below:

Begin by putting the Raspbmc on the SD Card

Before you can connect your Raspberry Pi to a TV, you should have the Raspbmc installer already in your SD card. First, plug the SD card into the computer. In the case of Windows users, you can download the installer then run it on the desktop to have the Raspbmc on the SD card.

For Linux and Mac users, you will have to run some few extra commands; but they are easy. After you have the installer added to the SD card, unplug it and continue to the next step.

Connect the Raspberry Pi, Install Raspbmc

It is now time for you to connect your Raspberry Pi to the TV. Connect your HDMI cable to the TV, connect the Ethernet cable to the computer, insert the SD card into the Raspberry Pi, then connect the micro of your Micro USB power cable to the wall. After connection, expect it to boot automatically from the SD card, which will start the installation process.

You can now let the installer do its work. This will take only 15 to 25 minutes. Once done, it will reboot your XMBC.

Configuration

Now that your XBMC is up and running, you only need to change a number of settings and you will have everything running correctly. The following are the changes to make:

Resolution- you can find this in "Settings > System > Video Output." If you need to watch videos of 720p resolution, the value for this should be changed to 720p. With this, the system and the menus will feel somewhat snappier.

- Overscan- you can find this in "Settings > System > Video Output > Video Calibration." If the XBMC window is not able to fit on your screen, you will have to change the calibrations for your video so they can fit.

- System Performance Profile- you can find this by navigating through "Programs > Raspbmc Settings > System Configuration." This is a setting for the Raspberry Pi which will make it possible for you to overlock the device. After this, everything will be running smoothly and in the right manner. It will be good to use the "Fast" option which help you speed up everything and the stability will remain fine. The setting for "Super" will give a fast speed, but there is a problem as it will create instability.

- MPEG2 Codec License- you should buy this from Raspberry Pi store, then enable it by navigating through "Programs > Raspbmc Settings > System Configuration." With this setting enabled, you will be able to play the MPEG-2 videos, which are the videos your Pi is unable to play out of box. However, if you don't intend to play these types, feel free to skip this step.

You will then be done with the needed configuration, so you can add some videos to your library, install any necessary add-ons, and customize the setup!

Chapter 5 - Building a Retro Game Console

You can use your Raspberry Pi 3 to make a retro game console in a few minutes. To do this, you should first install the operating system on an SD card then perform some simple file sharing from your PC.

To emulate the old-school video games, you should have two things. You should have game ROMS as well as an emulator for playing them. A ROM refers to a piece of a game which can be found on the device. The emulator should be used for playing the ROM.

The emulator ethics rule requires that one have a physical copy of the game if you are using the ROM. You can also create one from old cartridges.

The Raspberry Pi will automatically boot onto the EmulationStation. The programs runs off the custom SD card named RetroPie which allows you to make use of a controller to choose a game and an emulator without having to touch a mouse or keyboard. Once everything has been setup as expected, you will be able to navigate through the Pi and do everything from the controller.

Other than games, you will also be granted full access to media center software called Kodi. You will need to get into the advanced settings to download it. With this, you will have an all-in-one center for entertainment, running classic games and the media center.

Requirements

In this chapter, you should have the following:

1. **A Raspberry Pi**
   We will be using the Raspberry Pi 3. You will have full
   compatibility with the game and built-in Bluetooth and Wi-Fi.

2. **A micro USB power supply**

3. **An 8GB Micro SD Card, or a large-size one.**

4. **USB game controllers** (optional)

5. **USB keyboard**
   This will help you perform initial setup and if you need to
   configure the Wi-Fi.

6. **AV/HDMI, TV/monitor cables**

7. **A Mac/Windows/Linux computer**
   for setting up the SD cards and transferring the ROMS.

Once you have assembled the above components, follow the steps given
below:

Install RetroPie on SD Card

Due to the work of the RetroPie, the installation of the emulators on the
Raspberry Pi is easy. Follow the steps below:

Download RetroPie Project SD card image for the version of your Raspberry Pi, which should be either the 0/B/B+ or the 2/3. In this chapter, we will be using the version 3.7. However, the sucker might take a long time to perform the download based on the level of server activity.

1. After the download is complete, extract your image to your SD card by following a similar approach for a normal Raspbian image. In the case of Windows users, this is easy when you use the Win32DiskManager. For Mac users, make use of the RPI-sd card builder. For Linux users, you can use the terminal.

2. Once done, unplug the SD card from the computer and put it on your Raspberry Pi.

This is enough for the initial setup. For those planning to use the mouse and the keyboard other than the controller, you are almost done, so you can skip a number of steps and begin to transfer the ROM files.

If you prefer doing a manual installation of the emulators, just go ahead and do this. However, it will take a long time, usually about 9 hours to download and do the complete installation. However, with this method, you will be running the latest version of the emulators and you will be able to choose what needs to be installed.

Start the Raspberry Pi 3

In this step, you should boot your Raspberry Pi 3, then setup the EmulationStation. Plug the keyboard and one of the controllers to your Raspberry Pi 3. Insert the SD card that you had just burned. After some minutes of the automatic setup have elapsed, the Raspberry will boot automatically onto the EmulationStation as well as the interface wrapper, and it will have all your emulators on it. This where you will set the controller up and do a few changes for the system to work well.

Once it boots for the first time, follow the onscreen instructions to setup the controller. For those using a Bluetooth controller, this is the best time to connect it with the USB cable. You can then setup its Bluetooth in next step.

Once done, use your controller to navigate through the RetroPie. The controllers should be able to work with all your emulators as well as on the RetroPie. Other than the control of the basic movement, you will get some Hot Keys which can be used to accomplish certain actions within the game. These include:

- Select+Start: Exit a game

- Select+Left Shoulder: Load

- Select+Right Shoulder: Save

- Select+Right: Input State Slot Increase

- Select+X: RGUI Menu

- Select+Left: Input State Slot Decrease

- Select+B: Reset

All the above keys may not be useful, but it is good for you to know how to quit a game, create, save, as well as how to load a save.

It is also beneficial for you to note that even the RetroPie comes with many emulators; and it will hide the ones which do not have the games already installed. This means that as you scroll the RetroPie for the first time, you will not see emulators. The rest of the emulators will be shown when you are adding the games.

Setup the Wi-Fi

The new RetroPie has a in-built system that can allow you to access all the Raspberry Pi settings and tweak the memory from the EmulationStation. The majority of the settings are for advanced users, but it is wise for you to know how to setup the Wi-Fi.

The following steps will help:

1. Scroll down to option for "Configure WiFi," then tap the "A" button.

2. Choose "Connect to WiFi Network" and select your network. Enter the password and choose okay.

That is the base setup and the place from where you can do other changes. You can go ahead and edit the theme for Retropie, set the controller for Bluetooth, manage the files, etc.

Transfer ROMs from Primary Computer

Our assumption in this section is that you have a number of ROMs on your primary computer which you need to move to the Raspberry Pi 3.

Ensure the Raspberry Pi 3 is on and already connected to the router.

If connected, the RetroPie folder will appear as a shared folder automatically in your network. If this doesn't happen, you can go ahead and load it manually. For Windows users, launch the file manager then type "\\retropie" into folder location. For Mac users, launch the finder then choose "Go > Connect to Server." Type "smb://retropie," then click on Connect.

Now, it will become easy for you to copy the ROMS from your computer to the Pi remotely, so you should not be worried if you need to add more. After you are done with the file transfer, just reboot the Pi.

If you need using a USB Drive having ROMS, go ahead and use it.

2

Part 2: Projects with The Raspberry Pi & Python

Chapter 6 - Programming with Python on Raspberry Pi 3

The Raspberry Pi is a basic tool that can introduce anyone from anywhere in the world to computer programming. The Linux distribution for Raspberry Pi, which is Raspbian, comes with in-built programming languages and IDLEs, which will can help you get started with programming even after powering on the device for the first time.

Python is a very popular programming language across the world. It is highly supported in web applications, desktops, and other utilities. It is the best language for you to learn especially if you are new to programming.

> If you are using the latest version of the Raspbian OS, you are lucky as it comes with in-build tools for Python 3.3 and Python 2.x. The latest version of the Python is Python 3.x.

The Command Line and the IDE

To program with Python in the Raspberry Pi 3, you can choose to use either the Integrated Development Environment (IDE) or the terminal, and this will be determined with what you are comfortable. Python has an IDE named IDLE. In this case, we will be exploring the Python 3 IDLE.

To launch the Python 3 IDLE in Python, you just need to click it as shown below:

This will give you the Python shell and will allow you to work with Python in an interactive manner.

However, you may need to use Python from the terminal of your Raspberry Pi 3. To do this, just open this terminal and type the "python3" command. The Python command line will then be presented from which you will be able to run your Python scripts.

We will now demonstrate how you can interact with this terminal. Just type the following then hit the Enter key:

```
>>> 1+ 3
```

Once you hit the Enter key, you will get the sum of 1 and 3, which is 4. Again, type the following on the command line:

```
name = "John"
print (name)
```

Hit the enter key and you will get the value of name, which is John. The screenshot given below demonstrates:

```
>>> name = "john"
>>> print (name)
john
>>>
```

Write the example given below on the command line:

```
print ("Hello, Raspberry Pi 3 is good")
```

Hit the enter key on the keyboard. You will see the statement within the quotes printed on the terminal as shown below:

```
>>> print ("Hello, Raspberry Pi 3 is good")
Hello, Raspberry Pi 3 is good
>>>
```

Updating Python Packages

Python provides you with packages you can use to accomplish a variety of functionalities in your apps. You must install these packages in your local development environment.

The Raspbian Archives provides you with a few packages. The best way to get the packages is by running the "apt-get" commands as shown below:

```
sudo apt-get update
sudo apt-get install <python-package-name>
```

In the first command given above, we are updating the system to ensure that we can get all the updates available. In the second command, the <python-package-name> should be replaced with the name of the package you need to install in your system.

It is good for you to note that the Raspbian Archives do not provide all the Python packages. In such a case, you should use the Python Pip package management system. A good example is the "requests" package that makes it possible for the Python apps to work with the HTTP call functionality. The following command will help install this package:

```
$ pip3 install requests
```

If you need to see the details for the package we have just installed, just run the following command:

```
$ pip show requests
```

You will see details regarding the package.

GPIO Programming

The Raspberry Pi 3 can be used with other types of hardware for the creation of amazing electronic projects. The Pi 3 device itself provides you with 40 GPIO pins that you can use to interface with other types of hardware. You can receive data from these devices or write to them. This means that with the GPIO pins, it is possible to create apps which can write as well as control devices such as turning them on and off.

For you to be able to program the GPIO pins for your Raspberry Pi, you must use the GPIO python library for the Raspberry Pi. The following command will help you to install this library for the Python 3:

```
sudo apt-get install python3-rpi.gpio
```

The command will install the library so you can use it to create some simple applications. However, it is good for you to know that if you are using the latest version of the Raspbian OS, then this library comes pre-installed. In this case, you only have to update it by running the "sudo apt-get update" command.

Let us give an example demonstrating how this library can be used.

Open your Leafpad text editor, then save the sketch with the name "inputSketch.py." First, add the following statement to the file to import the library:

```
import RPi.GPIO as GPIO
```

Then specify the type of numbering system to be used to create the sketch. This can be done using the following code:

```
#set up the GPIO by use of BCM numbering
GPIO.setmode(GPIO.BCM)
```

```
#setup the GPIO by use of Board numbering
GPIO.setmode(GPIO.BOARD)
```

Note that a difference exists between the two types of numbering systems. With the BOARD numbering system, the pins will be used and numbered in the exact way they have been arranged or laid on the board. In the case of the BCM option, the Broadcom SoC numbering system is used. The BCM numbering system is the same for all programming languages, so we will be using it in this example.

Building a Circuit

We now get to the inputs and outputs. We will wire two momentary switches to the GPIO pins, that is, 23 and 24, which on the board are the pins 16 and 18. The switch on the pin 23 has been tied to a 3.3V, while the switch on the pin 24 has been placed on the ground. The reason for this is that the Raspberry Pi has both internal pull-up and the pull-down resistors, and you can specify these during the pin declarations.

You can then set the pins by writing the following:

```
GPIO.setup(23, GPIO.IN, pull_up_down=GPIO.PUD_DOWN)
GPIO.setup(24, GPIO.IN, pull_up_down=GPIO.PUD_UP)
```

With the above code, a pull-down resistor will be enabled on pin 23, while a pull-up resistor will be enabled on pin 24. It is now time for you to check to know whether you are able to read them. What the Pi is doing is looking for some high voltage on the pin 23 and for some low voltage on the pin 24. These should also be kept in a loop so that it can check for the pin voltage constantly.

Change your program to look like this:

```
import RPi.GPIO as GPIO
GPIO.setmode(GPIO.BCM)
GPIO.setup(23, GPIO.IN, pull_up_down = GPIO.PUD_DOWN)
GPIO.setup(24, GPIO.IN, pull_up_down = GPIO.PUD_UP)

while True:
    if(GPIO.input(23) == 1):
        print("Button 1 has been pressed")
    if(GPIO.input(24) == 0):
        print("Button 2 has been pressed")

GPIO.cleanup() #attention!
```

When using loops in Python, the indents are very important, so make sure that you indent your code correctly. If you need to access the GPIO pins, you must run your script using the "sudo" command. The command for running the script is as shown below:

```
sudo python inputSketch.py
```

To end the program, press CTRL+C on your keyboard.

The command *GPIO.cleanup()* used at the end of the program will be used to reset your pins to normal once you exit the program. If you fail to do this, then your GPIO pins will remain in the state you had set them the last time. However, in our little example, the cleanup code is never executed. Can you see why?

How to clean up correctly

If you are dealing with GPIO in your program, always make sure to call *GPIO.cleanup()* at the end. In the design of our programs, we use what's called an enless loop. You can see it in the code example above. The expression "True" is an always will be true until the end of the universe. So "while True" means, that the loop itself would never stop executing.

Only the interrupt we send to the program by pressing CTRL+C kills the program. The problem is, that the program is really "killed", so the code after the while-loop will never be executed. To solve this problem, we introduce a try/except/finally structure like this:

```
import RPi.GPIO as GPIO
GPIO.setmode(GPIO.BCM)
GPIO.setup(23, GPIO.IN, pull_up_down = GPIO.PUD_DOWN)
GPIO.setup(24, GPIO.IN, pull_up_down = GPIO.PUD_UP)

try:
    while True:
        if(GPIO.input(23) == 1):
            print("Button 1 has been pressed")
        if(GPIO.input(24) == 0):
            print("Button 2 has been pressed")
except KeyboardInterrupt:
    print('User terminated program by pressing CTRL+C')
finally:
    GPIO.cleanup()
```

When the user now presses CTRL+C the execution of the try-block (that contains the while-loop) is stopped and the except-block is being executed. The finally block is being executed in the end.

The cool thing about a finally block is, that whatever exception occurs during the execution of the code in the try-block, the finally block is *always* executed. There are a lot of possible exceptions, much more than just the KeyboardInterrupt exception. But whatever the occurring exception might be, the finally block is always being executed. Therefore, it is the right block to cleanup stuff. And we do that by calling GPIO.cleanup().

You can handle exceptions with the exception block, but you don't have to. It is perfectly fine to omit exception handling in our case and just use the try and finally blocks if we just want to cleanup resources. For the sake of simplicity, we will use just use the *try* and *finally* blocks in our future code examples. The above code without the exception block looks like this:

```
import RPi.GPIO as GPIO
GPIO.setmode(GPIO.BCM)
GPIO.setup(23, GPIO.IN, pull_up_down = GPIO.PUD_DOWN)
GPIO.setup(24, GPIO.IN, pull_up_down = GPIO.PUD_UP)

try:
    while True:
        if(GPIO.input(23) == 1):
            print("Button 1 has been pressed")
        if(GPIO.input(24) == 0):
            print("Button 2 has been pressed")
finally:
    GPIO.cleanup()
```

The Polling Problem

Our code is working, but it will print a line for every line after the button has been released. If you need to trigger an action or a command one time only, this will be inconvenient.

It is good that the GPIO library comes with a built-in falling-edge and rising-edge function. The rising-edge will be defined when the pin has changed from low to high, but only the change will be detected. The falling-edge represents the moment your pin will change from high to low.

Our code can be changed to reflect this:

```
import RPi.GPIO as GPIO

GPIO.setmode(GPIO.BCM)
GPIO.setup(23, GPIO.IN, pull_up_down = GPIO.PUD_DOWN)
GPIO.setup(24, GPIO.IN, pull_up_down = GPIO.PUD_UP)

try:
    while True:
        GPIO.wait_for_edge(23, GPIO.RISING)
        print("Button 1 has been Pressed")

        GPIO.wait_for_edge(23, GPIO.FALLING)
        print("Button 1 has been Released")

        GPIO.wait_for_edge(24, GPIO.FALLING)
        print("Button 2 Pressed")

        GPIO.wait_for_edge(24, GPIO.RISING)
        print("Button 2 has been Released")
finally:
    GPIO.cleanup()
```

After running the above code, you will notice that the statement will run only after detection of the edge has occurred. The reason for this is because Python waits for the edge to occur before it can move to the other part of the code. Note that we have written our code in a sequential manner, so the edges will occur in the same order we have written them.

Edge detection becomes useful when you need to wait for the input before you can proceed to the next part of the code. However, if you need to trigger a function by using some input device, then you should approach this using the events and callback functions as it is the best approach.

Events and Callback Functions

Suppose you have the camera module for the Raspberry and you need to use it to take a photo once you have pressed the button. However, you want to avoid the situation where your code will pull the button constantly, and you don't want to wait for too long for this to take place.

The use of a callback function gives us the best approach to run this code. The function has been attached to some specific GPIO pin and it will run whenever the edge has been detected. Try this with the following code:

```
import RPi.GPIO as GPIO

GPIO.setmode(GPIO.BCM)
GPIO.setup(23, GPIO.IN, pull_up_down = GPIO.PUD_DOWN)
GPIO.setup(24, GPIO.IN, pull_up_down = GPIO.PUD_UP)

def printFunction(channel):
    print("Button 1 has been pressed!")
    print("Note the way the bouncetime affects a button press")

try:
    GPIO.add_event_detect(23, GPIO.RISING, callback=printFunction,
bouncetime=300)

    while True:
        GPIO.wait_for_edge(24, GPIO.FALLING)
        print("Button has been 2 Pressed")

        GPIO.wait_for_edge(24, GPIO.RISING)
        print("Button has been 2 Released")
finally:
    GPIO.cleanup()
```

In this case, you will see that the button 1 will provoke the *printFunction* consistently, even as the main loop is waiting for the edge on button 2. The reason is because the callback function is contained in a different thread. Threads are of great importance in programming since they allow things to be done simultaneously without affecting anything in other functions.

When button 1 has been pressed, what will happen in our main loop will not be affected in any way.

Threads are also important; you can remove them as easily as adding them, which is shown below:

```
GPIO.remove_event_detect(23)
```

After, you will be free to add some different functions to the pin.

Adding the Functionality

The Raspberry Pi is not setup for PWM outputs or analog inputs. This is true despite the fact that callback functions are good for GPIO pins. However, since the Pi has both the Tx and Rx pins (pins 8, 10, GPIO 14, 15), communication with Arduino becomes easy.

If you are in need of a project that requires analog sensor input, or some smooth PWM output, you can simply do this by writing commands to serial port to Arduino.

Chapter 7 - Adding Electronics: The LED Project

In this section, we will be showing you how to light a LED.

What you need

Other than the Raspberry Pi, you should have the following:

- A breadboard
- An LED
- 330 ohm resistor
- Two male-female jumper wires

Breadboard

The breadboard will provide you with a way to connect your electronic components and you will not have to solder them together. We use them to test the design of a circuit before we can create a printed circuit board (PCB). The breadboard holes are usually connected in a certain pattern.

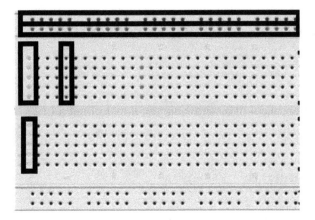

The holes in the top row are connected together. The same applies to the holes in the second row and the last 2 rows of the breadboard.

In the center area, there are 2 blocks of 5 lines of holes each. The holes of each column in each line are connected. In the image above, some of the connected holes are indicated with rectangles to help you get an idea of how it works.

At first, this might seem a bit strange, but actually this setup proves to be very convenient when designing circuits for prototyping.

LED

A LED (Light Emitting Diode) will light when electricity is passed through it.

After selecting a LED, you will realize that there is a leg that is longer than the other one. The longer leg is known as the anode, and it must be connected to the positive supply of your circuit. The shorter leg is known as the cathode and is connected to the negative side.

The LED will only work if you supply power in the correct order. Connecting them in the wrong way will make them fail to light but it will not break them.

The Resistor

Resistors are used when you need to connect your LEDs to the GPIO pins on your Raspberry Pi. Your Raspberry Pi is only capable of supplying a small current of about 60mA.

Note that your LEDs need more power than this, and they can burn your Pi. The purpose of resistors in the circuit is to ensure that only a small amount of current passes and that the Pi is not damaged. In this case, we will be using 300 ohms resistors that can be identified by their color codes.

Jumper wires

These are used on the breadboard to jump from one connection to another. You will be using those having different connectors at their ends.

Building the Circuit

The circuit will be made up of a power supply, which is the Pi, the LED which will light after power is passed, and a resistor for limiting the amount of power flowing in the circuit.

One of the ground pins will be used to act as the 0 or negative ends of the battery. A Gpio pin will provide us with the positive end for our battery. In this case, we will make use of the pin 18. If taken high, meaning the output will be of 3.3 volts, our LED will light. The connection should be done as shown below:

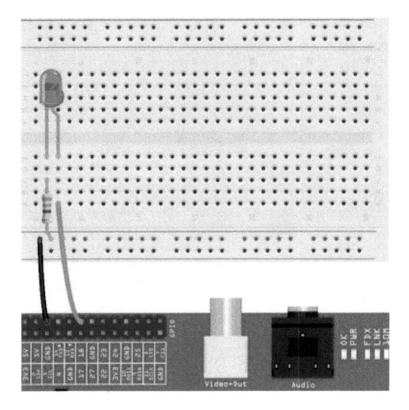

In the next step, just turn off the Pi if you short on something accidentally. You should use one jumper wire to connect the ground pin to the rail, which is marked with blue on the breadboard. The corresponding female end should then go to the pin of the Pi, while the male one to a hole on your breadboard.

The resistor should then be connected to the same row on the breadboard to a column.

The LED legs should then be pushed to the breadboard, while ensuring that the right leg is on the right. You can then complete the circuit by doing a connection of pin 18 to right your LED's right side leg.

Write the program

At this point, you are ready to create some code to help you switch on the LED. Turn on the Pi, then launch the terminal. You should create a new file named ""LED.py." Just type the following command on the terminal:

```
nano LED.py
```

Add the code given below to this file:

```
import RPi.GPIO as GPIO
import time

GPIO.setmode(GPIO.BCM)
GPIO.setwarnings(False)
GPIO.setup(18,GPIO.OUT)

print "LED is on"
GPIO.output(18,GPIO.HIGH)

time.sleep(1)

print "LED is off"
GPIO.output(18,GPIO.LOW)
```

After the code has been typed and checked, save and then exit the text editor by pressing "Ctrl + x" then "y," then hit the Enter key.

To run the code in the file, type the following command on the terminal:

```
sudo python LED.py
```

You should observe how the LED behaves. You will see it turn on for a second and it will then go off. In case you get an error, know that you have an error in your code, so open it in the anno text editor by running the command "nano LED.py," then edit it.

The "import RPi.GPIO as GPIO" statement helps to import the Raspberry GPIO library to our code as we want to use it. We are in need of pausing our script. This is why we have used the "import time" to import the "time" library which will help us achieve this.

We are also using different names for our pins. The "GPIO.setmode(GPIO.BCM)" statement will help the Python interpreter know the kind of numbering system we are using. The "GPIO.setwarnings(False)" statement helps us turn off the feature for printing warning messages on the screen.

The "GPIO.setup(18,GPIO.OUT)" statement has been used to tell the interpreter that pin at number 18 will be used for the purpose of displaying information.

The statement "print "LED is on" has been used to help print a message the screen. The Statement "GPIO.output(18,GPIO.HIGH)" helps turn on our GPIO pin. This is an indication that our pin has been made to provide a power of 3.3 volts. This voltage is enough to turn the LED on. The "time.sleep(1)" will help us pause the Python program for a second. The next line is simple as it helps print some information on the screen.

The statement "GPIO.output(18,GPIO.LOW)" helps to turn off our GPIO pin, which is an indication that it will no longer be supplying power.

At this point, you have achieved your target, which is to turn your LED on and off. Congratulations! With Python and Raspberry, you can enhance the functionality of your Pi device.

Chapter 8 - Creating a Photo Frame

The Photo Frame is a good way for you to view the photos of your loved ones or anything which you may need to show on a display. In this chapter, we will be creating a digital photo frame.

What you need

You will need the following equipment:

1. Raspberry Pi 3

2. A micro SD card

3. Wi-Fi dongle or ethernet cable

4. USB Drive or external hard drive

5. Screen (touch screen if available)

The following are also needed, but are optional:

6. USB keyboard

7. Raspberry Pi case

8. USB mouse

Setting up your photo frame

We will be using a Raspberry Pi touch screen, but feel free to make use of any screen you have. You only have to connect the Pi 3 to the screen via the HDMI port, DSI port, or by use of a custom HAT.

It is now time for us to setup the software for Photo Frame.

Our first setting will involve preventing the screen from going blank. This calls for us to implement a power setting on our Pi 3.

The feature which makes the screen go off should be changed in the "lightdm.conf" file. Open this file by running the following command:

```
sudo nano /etc/lightdm/lightdm.conf
```

The file will be opened in the nano editor. Identify the [SeatsDefaults] line, then add the following statement just below:

```
xserver-command=X -s 0 -dpms
```

The file should be as shown below:

```
GNU nano 2.2.6          File: /etc/lightdm/lightdm.conf

SeatDefaults]
server-command=X -s
type=xlocal
xdg-seat=seat0
pam-service=lightdm
pam-autologin-service=lightdm-autologin
pam-greeter-service=lightdm-greeter
xserver-command=X
xserver-layout=
xserver-config=
xserver-allow-tcp=false
xserver-share=true
xserver-hostname=
xserver-display-number=
xdmcp-manager=
xdmcp-port=177
xdmcp-key=
unity-compositor-command=unity-system-compositor
unity-compositor-timeout=60
```

You can then press "ctrl + x" followed by "y" to save and exit the file.

You can reboot the device, and you will observe that you screen will not go off even after 10 minutes of being inactive. The device can be rebooted by executing the command:

```
sudo reboot
```

You may need to set it up to be in a position to drag and drop images into your Pi 3. In such a case, you must setup a network-attached storage. Thus, you will be able to setup s folder that can be found on a local network. It will also be good to setup SSH (Secure Shell) so you can access the device even as the slideshow continues. You don't have an easy way to exit the slideshow unless you choose to turn the device on and off, and you don't have it start automatically.

We will be using the *feh* package to setup the slideshow. It is a cataloguer and an image viewer. This image viewer will not get bogged down even when you have huge GUI dependencies. We are using it because it is lightweight and has no major complications.

Run the following command to install the package:

```
sudo apt-get install feh
```

It is now time to test whether this package is working as expected. You can achieve this by running the command given below. Ensure that you replace the "/media/NICDD1/test" with the directory where you have stored your image. Here is the command:

```
DISPLAY=:0.0 XAUTHORITY=/home/pi/.Xauthority /usr/bin/feh --quiet --
preload --randomize --full-screen --reload 60 -Y --slideshow-delay 15.0
/media/NICDD1/test
```

We can now make our command to shorter by using some shorter tags as the following demonstrates:

```
DISPLAY=:0.0 XAUTHORITY=/home/pi/.Xauthority /usr/bin/feh -q -p -Z -F -
R  60 -Y -D 15.0 /media/NICDD1/test
```

You will notice that the command line bar will be locked because you have typed a long-running command. To send it to the background, just type the & sign.

We should now go ahead and store it in some a script file. This can be added or even changed later. The file can be made by running the command below:

```
sudo nano /home/pi/picture-frame.sh
```

In this case, we have named the file "picture-frame.sh." You can then add the lines given below to your file:

```
#!/bin/bash
DISPLAY=:0.0 XAUTHORITY=/home/pi/.Xauthority /usr/bin/feh -q -p -Z -F -
R  60 -Y -D 15.0 /media/NICDD1/test
```

It is now time for you to run the script to test whether it is working. Just run the command:

```
bash /home/pi/picture-frame.sh
```

We need to make this script begin to run during boot time. Since you have the SSH enabled, it is possible to access the Pi from a remote location when you are unable to access the screen or the GUI. You should ensure that this has been done before boot time. You can run the following command to open the "rc.local" file:

```
sudo nano /etc/rc.local
```

You can then identify the "exit 0" command add the following commands below:

```
sleep 10
bash /home/picture-frame.sh &
```

If you need to kill the process to access the screen again, just run the following command:

```
sudo pkill feh
```

You should now be able to see a slideshow of your images. In case any errors are experienced, doublecheck the steps and make corrections on any errors made.

Chapter 9 - Installing Magic Mirror on Raspberry Pi 3

Magic Mirror refers to a webpage which runs on the web server in your Raspberry Pi. We will be showing you how to set this up.

What you need

You should have the following:

1. Raspberry Pi 3

2. USB mouse

3. A 2A Raspberry Pi power supply

4. Raspberry Pi 3 case

5. MicroSD card reader

6. MicroSD card, 32GB

7. HDMI cable

Hands on

You should have installed Raspbian OS in your Pi, which will allow us to run both Jasper and MagicMirror. Raspbian Jessy is the best for the purposes of this chapter. You can get its image from the archives then burn it to your SD card.

Boot the Pi

Now that you have OS on the SD card, unplug it from the computer and plug it to the Raspberry Pi. Connect the mouse, Wifi USB adapter, keyboard, HDMI cable, and the power cable for your Pi. If you are taken to the shell rather than to the command line, just type the following command to be taken to the GUI:

```
startx
```

The MagicMirror expects that your Pi is Wifi-enabled so that connection to the Internet may be possible and remote access to it.

Click on the network icon located on top right corner of the screen, choose your Wi-Fi, then type in the password and click Ok.

Remote Connection

You can now establish a remote connection to your Pi from your computer. Launch the terminal or the command prompt from either Mac or Windows and type the following command:

```
ssh pi@your-pis-ip-address
```

If you are asked to enter the password, type the default password for your Raspberry Pi.

Configure the Raspbian

It is always good to change the default password for your Pi. Type the following command, then hit the Enter key:

```
passwd
```

The filesystem of your Pi should be expanded so that it can fill all of the available space and boot into the GUI. Again, type the following command, then hit the Enter key:

```
sudo raspi-config
```

Choose Expand FileSystem and press the Enter key.

In the next step, we will our Pi to boot into Raspbian GUI for the Chromium kiosk mode. To do this, choose Enable Boot to Desktop Scratch, then select Desktop Log In. Highlight the choice and use the Tab to get to then hit the Enter key.

Tab over to, hit Enter and reboot your Pi by running the command below:

```
sudo reboot
```

You can run the commands given below to update the Pi:

```
sudo apt-get update
sudo apt-get upgrade -yes
```

Install Chromium

Chromium is simply a web browser that we will be configuring to run it as a kiosk, as it will provide the interface for Magic Mirror.

It is now time for us to download and install the necessary packages. If you are using the Wheezy version, run the following command:

```
sudo apt-get install chromium x11-xserver-utils unclutter
```

For those using the Jessie version, run the following commands:

```
wget http://ftp.us.debian.org/debian/pool/main/libg/libgcrypt11/libgcrypt11_1.5.0-
5+deb7u3_armhf.deb

wget http://launchpadlibrarian.net/218525709/chromium-browser_45.0.2454.85-
0ubuntu0.14.04.1.1097_armhf.deb

wget http://launchpadlibrarian.net/218525711/chromium-codecs-ffmpeg-
extra_45.0.2454.85-0ubuntu0.14.04.1.1097_armhf.deb

sudo dpkg -i libgcrypt11_1.5.0-5+deb7u3_armhf.deb

sudo dpkg -i chromium-codecs-ffmpeg-extra_45.0.2454.85-
0ubuntu0.14.04.1.1097_armhf.deb

sudo dpkg -i chromium-browser_45.0.2454.85-
0ubuntu0.14.04.1.1097_armhf.deb
```

The commands will install all the necessary packages for you.

Installing Apache

The dashboard for Magic Mirror is a webpage, so a web server is needed to host the dashboard. This calls for us to install the Apache server by running the following command:

```
sudo apt-get install apache2 apache2-doc apache2-utils
```

The following command will help you add the support for PHP:

```
sudo apt-get install libapache2-mod-php5 php5 php-pear php5-xcache
```

Restart your Pi for the changes to take effect:

```
sudo reboot
```

After the Pi reboots, the changes made will take effect.

Installing the Interface

There are several dashboards that can be used for Magic Mirror. However, we only need one, so let's go ahead and install it.

Change to the webroot directory:

```
cd /var/www
```

In the case of Jessie, the web root can be the "/var/www/html."

We can then clone the MichMich's MagicMirror repository. The following command will help achieve this:

```
sudo git clone https://github.com/MichMich/MagicMirror.git
```

This will give us the dashboard that we will be using. You can move files to webroot then remove the old ones as demonstrated below:

```
cd MagicMirror
sudo mv * ..
cd ..
sudo rm -rf MagicMirror
```

At this point, it is possible to open the IP address of your PI on the computer's browser, and you will see the dashboard for MagicMirror.

Customizing the Interface

We can now configure the interface to meet our needs. You only have to open the following file in text editor:

```
sudo nano js/config.js
```

You should then change the language from the top to reflect your language. I will be using English:

```
lang: 'en',
Updating Weather Settings
```

The weather settings should be changed to reflect your location (weather.params.q), language (weather.params.lang), and preferred unit (weather.params.units). My configuration is as shown below:

```
params: {
    q: 'Tampa,Florida',
    units: 'imperial',
    lang: 'en',
    APPID: 'THE_FREE_OPENWEATHER_API_KEY'
}
```

Open the URL http://openweathermap.org/appid on your browser to generate a free API key, then paste it.

MagicMirror also spins on a number of complements determined by the time of the day. The complements can be changed to something else if there is a need .

MagicMirror will also show the default public iCal calendar that shows soccer or football matches. Changes can be made by pasting the public URL of the calendar. After you are finished with the configuration, just save it and exit.

Run Chromium in Kiosk Mode

At this step, we will be configuring chromium so it can run in Kiosk mode. Launch autostart config file in your Nano editor. The config file for wheezy should be opened using the following command:

```
sudo nano /etc/xdg/lxsession/LXDE-pi/autostart
```

For the case of Jessie, this should be done as shown below:

```
sudo nano ~/.config/lxsession/LXDE-pi/autostart
```

It is also good to disable the screensaver. In both Wheezy and Jessie, you only must add the hash (#) symbol to the beginning of the following statement, as shown below, as a way of commenting it:

```
# @xscreensaver -no-splash
```

Our aim is to have the Chromium startup while in Kiosk mode. If you are using Wheezy, add the lines given below to the bottom of the file:

```
@xset s off
@xset -dpms
@xset s noblank
@unclutter -idle 1
/usr/bin/chromium --kiosk --ignore-certificate-errors --disable-restore-session-state "http://localhost"
```

For Jessie users, add the lines below to the bottom of the file:

```
@xset s off
@xset -dpms
@xset s noblank
@unclutter -idle 1
@chromium-browser --incognito --kiosk http://localhost/
```

To exit the file, just press Ctrl-x, type y, then hit enter key. We should go ahead and modify the BIOS settings for our Pi.

Run the following command to open the BIOS configuration settings:

```
sudo nano /boot/config.txt
```

The display should be rotated for 90 degrees. This can be accomplished by adding the line given below:

```
display_rotate=1
```

If you need to rotate for 270 degrees in the other direction, add the following line:

```
display_rotate=3
```

Enabling HDML Hotplugging

To enable this, identify the following line and then uncomment by removing the hash (#) symbol before it:

```
| hdmi_force_hotplug=1
```

Just save then exit the file, and reboot your Pi for the changes to take effect.

```
| sudo reboot
```

At this point, the setup for MagicMirror is working, and it will be good for you to create backup for the SD card. Although this is optional, it is wise in any case something negative occurs during the installation of Jasper; and it will be possible for you to revert.

Chapter 10 - Adding Voice Control to Raspberry Pi

This will be done using Jasper. It is an open-source and voice-controlled platform that runs on many systems including the Raspberry Pi. You can use Jasper to build an application that can be controlled by voice for adding things to the Google Calendar, playing Spotify playlists, and even automating your entire home.

In this chapter, we will help you setup Jasper on your Raspberry Pi 3 and enable it to make commands to do things.

What you need

Ensure you have the following:

1. Ethernet cable

2. USB microphone

3. Raspberry Pi 3

4. MicroSD card, 32GB

5. MicroSD card reader

6. Stereo speakers

7. 2A Raspberry Pi power supply

8. Raspberry Pi 3 case

Ensure that your Raspberry Pi 3 is setup with everything, including the Raspbian OS. Establish a remote connection via SSH.

Installing Jasper

For the users of Raspbian Jessie, you are provided with three options on installing the Jasper. These include manual, use of a disk image, and use of an install script.

Let us use an install script to setup this. Use the following command to obtain the Jasper for the Jessie install script:

```
cd ~/
wget https://raw.githubusercontent.com/Howchoo/raspi-
helpers/master/scripts/jasper-installer.sh
```

The script has the name "jasper-installer.sh." You can then use the **sudo** command to run your install script as shown below:

```
sudo chmod +x jasper-installer.sh
sudo ./jasper-installer.sh
```

Note that we first created an executable of the file, and we then executed it in the above command. You will see a message welcoming you to the script. You will be prompted to select STT support, which can be Network or Local. If you are sure your Pi will be connected to the Internet at all times, then choose Network; otherwise, choose Local. In my case, I will choose Network.

Set up the network

The installation pf dependencies will begin, which can take some time, so be patient.

You may get the error given below:

```
Could not open requirements file: [Errno 2] No such file or directory:
'/root/jasper/client/requirements.txt'
```

Troubleshoot this by running the following commands:

```
sudo chmod +x ~/jasper/client/requirements.txt
sudo pip install --upgrade -r ~/jasper/client/requirements.txt
```

The commands will work by reading the required packages for Jasper from requirements.txt and then upgrade/install them as expected.

Creating Jasper User File

It is now time for us to set up the Jasper user profile. The information provided in this case will help us set up various integrations, the localization results, and other things. Change your directory, then create the file by running the following commands:

```
cd ~/jasper/client
python populate.py
```

Type in the profile information you need, which can be first name, last name, phone number, email address, time zone, etc. The profile will be used in specific add-ons that will provide data such as weather, text message alerts, email notifications, and more. You should then choose whether you will receive the notifications via email or text.

You may be prompted to choose the Speech to Text (STT) engine you would like to use. PocketSphinx is the best for you, so you only need to enter the following command and hit Enter:

```
sphinx
```

Run Jasper

You can type the command given below to run Jasper:

```
python /usr/local/lib/jasper/jasper.py
```

Note that Raspbian might have been installed in a different directory; if you get a "not found" message, try the following:

```
python /home/pi/jasper/jasper.py
```

To make Jasper start during startup, use the following:

```
crontab -e
```

Note that we have used cron, used for job scheduling, you can then add the following line of code:

```
@reboot python /usr/local/lib/jasper/jasper.py;
```

Save your file, exit it, then reboot by running the command below:

```
sudo reboot
```

Afterward, you will be able to issue commands to your Jasper and it will respond to them accordingly.

Troubleshooting

You may get an error related to the one given below:

```
RuntimeError: hmm_dir
'/usr/local/share/pocketsphinx/model/hmm/en_US/hub4wsj_sc_8k' does not
exist! Please make sure that you have set the correct hmm_dir in your
profile.
```

In this case, you only must open the "stt.py" file by running the following command:

```
vim /usr/local/lib/jasper/client/stt.py
```

The file will be opened in Vim text editor. Look for the following line:

```
    def __init__(self, vocabulary, hmm_dir="/usr/local/share/" +
                "pocketsphinx/model/hmm/en_US/hub4wsj_sc_8k"):
```

You can then change the line to the following:

```
    def __init__(self, vocabulary, hmm_dir="/usr/share/" +
                "pocketsphinx/model/hmm/en_US/hub4wsj_sc_8k"):
```

Note that the change involves only removing the word "local."

Conclusion

We have come to end of this guide. The Raspberry Pi 3 is a great device, and you can do a lot with it. You can use the Raspberry Pi 3 as a media server, and you can play music with it. You can also use it to run your images or pictures in the form of a slide show. The beneficial aspect of the Raspberry Pi 3 is that it can be programmed with common programming languages such as Python. For instance, you can program its GPIO pins to help you switch the LEDs on and off.

Thank you!

Thank you for buying this book. If you enjoyed reading this text and developing all the fun projects, then I'd like to ask you for a favor. **Would you be kind enough to leave a review on Amazon?**

It'd be greatly appreciated!

All my best wishes,

Steve

www.ingramcontent.com/pod-product-compliance
Lightning Source LLC
Chambersburg PA
CBHW070854070326
40690CB00009B/1832